Words to Whisper Words to Shout

and other poems to read aloud

For Bretton Hall tutors
John and Annita

First published in Great Britain in 2002 by

Belitha Press
A member of **Chrysalis** Books plc
64 Brewery Road, London N7 9NT

Series editors: Pie Corbett, Mary-Jane Wilkins
Editor: Russell Mclean
Designer: Sarah Goodwin

ISBN 1 84138 261 2 (hardback)
ISBN 1 84138 263 9 (paperback)

British Library Cataloguing in Publication Data
for this book is available from the British Library.

Printed by Omnia Books Ltd, Glasgow

10 9 8 7 6 5 4 3 2 1 (hb)
10 9 8 7 6 5 4 3 2 1 (pb)

Words to Whisper Words to Shout

and other poems to read aloud

Compiled by Michaela Morgan
Illustrated by Chloë Cheese · 154732x

Belitha Press

Contents

Words to Whisper

Words to whisper...
Words to **SHOUT**.
To pack a punch!
To cast a doubt...
Words to relish
Words to chew.
Antique words
or words brand new.
Words to clacker and to clack
like trains that travel on a track.
Words to soothe, words to sigh
to shush and hush and *lullaby*.
Words to tickle or to tease
to murmur, hum or buzz like bees.
Words like hubbub, splash and splutter
wiffle, waffle, murmur, mutter.
Words that babble like a stream
Words to **SNAP!** when you feel mean.

Get lost! Drop dead! Take a hike!
Shut it! Beat it! On your bike!
Cruel words that taint and taunt.
Eerie words that howl and haunt.
Words with rhythm. Words with rhyme.
Words to make you feel just fine.
To clap your hands, tap your feet
or click your fingers to the beat.
Words to make you grow – or cower.
Have you heard the word?

WORDPOWER

Michaela Morgan

What Do You Do with a Didgeridoo?

What do you do with a didgeridoo?
A didgeri, didgeri, didgeridoo?
You blow in one end and make it go **WOOOH!**
That's what you do with a didgeridoo,
You blow in one end and make it go **WOOOH!**

What do you do with electric guitars?
Electric, electric, electric guitars?
You **CRASH** 'em and **BASH** 'em and play 'em in bars!
That's what you do with electric guitars,
You **CRASH** 'em and **BASH** 'em and play 'em in bars!

What do you do with a big double bass?
A big double, big double, big double bass?
You go **DUM! DUM! DUM!** and you screw up your face!
That's what you do with a big double bass,
You go **DUM! DUM! DUM!** and you screw up your face!

What do you do with a mandolin string?
A mandolin, mandolin, mandolin string?
You pluck it and pick it and make it go PING!
That's what you do with a mandolin string,
You pluck it and pick it and make it go PING!

What do you do at the end of the show?
The end of, the end of, the end of the show?
You stand up and smile and get ready to go!
That's what you do at the end of the show,
You stand up and smile and get ready to go!

And what do you do if the crowd shouts for **MORE**?

You go...

Didgeridoo – make it go **WOOOH!**
Electric guitars – play 'em in bars!
Big double bass – screw up your face!
Mandolin string – make it go PING!
End of the show – get ready to go!

Then you nod and you bow
And the audience shouts **WOW!**

Nick Penny

The Bee's Story

'Buzz! Buzz!' said the bee.
If you listen to the flea
Or the pretty butterfly
Or the spotty ladybird
You would never ever know
That they're flitter flying by
And you'll maybe wonder why
I buzz.
Now mosquitoes have a whine
And a whine is very fine
And the beetles sometimes click
And the death watch beetles tick
But a bee will always buzz.
It's what we does.
We **BUZZ!**

And it may be 'cos we're busy
Busy buzzing to and fro
And we buzz around for hours
As we pollinate the flowers
(Don't you think, if we're so busy
We should **BIZZ** instead of
BUZZ?
Maybe someone couldn't spell –
Who can tell?)
And we're busy being **BUZZY**
Every day
So when you hear somebody say
'What a busy little bee'
Think of me.
Buzz buzz.
It's what we does.

Vivian French

Mrs Sprockett's Strange Machine

Mrs Sprockett has a strange machine.
It will thrill you through and through.
It's got wheels and springs and seven strings
And this is what they do.

Pull string number one...
...it begins to hum mmmm mmmmmmmm
Pull string number two...
...it goes **COCK A DOODLE DOO**.
Pull string number three...
...it will buzz like a bee zzzzzzzzzzzz
Pull string number four...
...it will start to **ROAR**.
Pull string number five...
...it will dip and dive.
Pull string number six...
...it will play silly tricks.
Pull string number seven...
...it will fly up to heaven.

Mrs Sprockett has a strange machine.
It will thrill you through and through.
It's got wheels and springs and seven strings
And ... **I WISH I HAD ONE TOO!**

Michaela Morgan

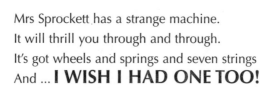

My Old Man

My old man plays football
he wears a football shirt
he's got the latest colours
and he's always covered in dirt

He looks a proper nar-nar
in his great big football boots
they're much too big for his little feet
that's why he overshoots

When my old man plays football
upon a windy day
he has to hold his hair on
in case it blows away

He's also so short-sighted
he shouldn't play at all
he needs a magnifying glass
to help him see the ball

He wants to be the captain
but he can't run very far
before he needs a stretcher
and a ride home in the car

So if you see a player
looking all pale and sad
don't kick him off the football pitch
it might be my old dad

Andrea Shavick

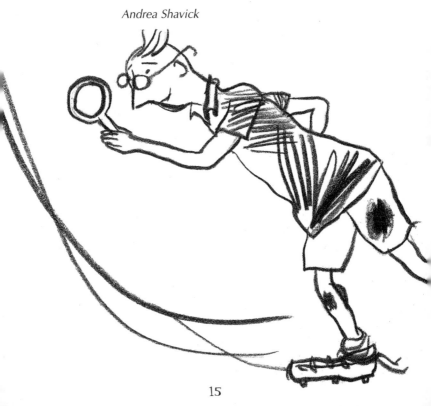

Crocodile under my Bed

There's a crocodile under my bed, Mum says,
and if I get up before seven o'clock
he'll bite my legs off.

The sun breaks through the curtains
like a burglar cracking a safe,
and the birds start shouting
from their start-the-morning place,
but I can't get up, not yet.
There's a crocodile under my bed.

There's a crocodile under my bed, Mum says,
and if I'm too early putting my feet on the floor
I won't have feet any more.

So after the story, after the kiss,
when the house falls quiet around the drone
of a lone TV, there's just him and me.
He forms from shadows and bits of fluff:
his scaly scales and his toothy teeth
await beneath.

There's a crocodile under my bed, Mum says,
and he only lives there when it's night
and at other times it's quite all right.

When it's the middle of the night
and I need to pee
I can feel him breathing under me,
grinning his horrible toothy grin,
so I stay right where I am
and hold it in.

There's a crocodile under my bed, Mum said
when I was much younger, and easy to scare,
but there'll always be dark,
too much dark under there,
and I never forget what my mother said –
there's a crocodile under my bed.

Ros Barber

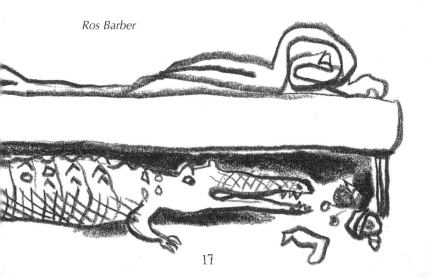

Monster Pie

'Yum,' says the monster,
What's for lunch?
A chewy stone
that I can crunch,
In a gravel and gravy pie.

'Yippee,' says the monster,
What's for lunch?
A chewy stone that I can crunch,
And a spiky stick
That I can lick,
In a gravel and gravy pie.

'Hurray,' says the monster,
What's for lunch?
A chewy stone that I can crunch,
And a spiky stick that I can lick,
And two little feet
That I can eat,
In a gravel and gravy pie.

'Hiccup,' says the monster,
What's for lunch?
A chewy stone that I can crunch,
And a spiky stick that I can lick,
And two little feet that I can eat,
A big soft pillow
That I can swallow,
In a gravel and gravy pie.

'Phew,' says the monster,
What's for lunch?
A chewy stone that I can crunch,
And a spiky stick that I can lick,
And two little feet that I can eat,
A big soft pillow that I can swallow,
A bright blue kite
That I will bite,
In a gravel and gravy pie.

'Oh no,' says the monster,
Here's the crunch,
I've eaten too much
For my lunch.
A chewy stone that I did crunch,
And a spiky stick that I did lick,
And two little feet that I did eat,
A big soft pillow that I did swallow,
A bright blue kite that I did bite,
In a gravel and gravy pie.

Then with a **splop!**
His tummy went **pop**,
And out flew his lunch:
A chewy stone that he did crunch,
And a spiky stick that he did lick,
And two little feet that he did eat,
A big soft pillow that he did swallow,
A bright blue kite that he did bite,
In a gravel and gravy pie.
Oh my! Oh my! Oh my!

Tom Murphy

Rat in the Attic

Rat-a-tat-tat. Rat-a-tat-tat.
Rat up in the attic. Oh, listen to that.
Rattling around like an acrobat.
That pitter-pattering, clattering rat.

Rat-a-tat-tat. Rat-a-tat-tat.
Rat-a-tat-tat. Drat that rat!
Rat-a-tat-tat. Get the prat!
That pitter-pattering, clattering rat.

Rat-a-tat-tat. Rat-a-tat-tat.
Flatten that rat! Batter the brat!
Splatter that un-get-at-able rat!
That pitter-pattering, clattering rat.

Rat-a-tat-tat. Rat-a-tat-tat.
Catch that rat. Beat it flat.
Beat it flat with a cricket bat.
That pitter-pattering, clattering rat.

Rat-a-tat-tat. Rat-a-tat-tat.
Rat up in the attic. Will you listen to that?
Rat-a-tat-tat. Rat-a-tat-tat.
Rat-a-tat-tat. Rat-a-tat-tat.
Rat-a-tat-tat. Rat-a-tat-tat.

Nick Toczek

Daredevil Gran

Shout out loud, say what you like
Great Gran is manic on her motorbike.
Shout out loud, say what you like
Great Gran is manic on her motorbike.

**Vroom vroom ooo, vroom vroom aaah
Vroom vroom eee**

Last week her helmet touched the stars
when she zoomed over thirty cars
she didn't quibble, didn't fuss
when they added a double-decker bus.

Shout out loud, say what you like
Great Gran is manic on her motorbike.
Shout out loud, say what you like
Great Gran is manic on her motorbike.

**Vroom vroom ooo, vroom vroom aaah
Vroom vroom eee**

She's a headline-hunting, bike-stunting
wacky-wild-one-woman-show,
she revs and roars to wild applause
there is no place her bike won't go.
She gives them shivers jumping rivers
and balancing across high wires
with a cheer she changes gear,
flies her bike through blazing tyres.

Shout out loud, say what you like
Great Gran is manic on her motorbike.
Shout out loud, say what you like
Great Gran is manic on her motorbike.

**Vroom vroom ooo, vroom vroom aaah
Vroom vroom eee**

She told me when she quits bike-riding
she's going to take up paragliding
I'll always be her greatest fan
My dazzling, daredevil Gran!

David Harmer

Silly Billy Banjo

Silly Billy Banjo plays his song,
high Billy Banjo, low Billy Banjo,
silly Billy Banjo plays his song,
high Billy, low Billy,
silly Billy Banjo.

Silly Billy Banjo plays his song,
quick Billy Banjo, s - l - o - w Billy Banjo,
silly Billy Banjo plays his song,
quick Billy, s - l - o - w Billy,
high Billy, low Billy,
silly Billy Banjo.

Silly Billy Banjo plays his song,
shhh Billy Banjo, **YO!** Billy Banjo,
silly Billy Banjo plays his song,
shhh Billy, **YO!** Billy,
quick Billy, s - l - o - w Billy,
high Billy, low Billy,
silly Billy Banjo.

Silly Billy Banjo plays his song,
STOP! Billy Banjo, GO! Billy Banjo,
silly Billy Banjo plays his song,
STOP! Billy, GO! Billy,
shhh Billy, **YO!** Billy,
quick Billy, s - l - o - w Billy,
high Billy, low Billy,
silly Billy Banjo.

High low high low
quick s - l - o - w quick s - l - o - w
shhh **YO!** shhh **YO!**   *(repeat three times,*
Stop! GO! Stop! GO!   *increasing speed)*

Silly Billy Banjo **stop**!
Silly Billy Banjo **stop**! **STOP! STOP!**

Nick Penny

25

Kit 10

If I meet a furry animal
it makes me wheeze.
My eyes begin to water.
I start to snuffle and to sneeze.
I've got an al – ler – gy.
I can't have a cat.
Gran said 'I can do something 'bout that!'
She went to her workshop
to hammer and to **bang**.
I heard a *whistle* and a *hissing*
a clatter and a **clang**,
a binging and a bonging,
a fizz, bang, **splat!**
Then Gran popped out with... Robocat.

It's a Robocat.
It has no fur.
It has metal whiskers.
It goes whirr whirr **WHIRR.**
It's my little metal kitty
it's not cuddly and pretty
but I love my little robocat.
I call it Kit 10.

It's got springy springs to bounce on,
to leap up high and pounce from.
It's got wheels like a scooter
and a funny honky hooter.
It can prowl and yowl and **HOWL**
but it cannot purr.
The softest sound it makes is
whirr whirr **WHIRR.**

It's a Robocat.
It has no fur.
It has metal whiskers.
It goes whirr whirr **WHIRR.**
It's my little metal kitty
it's not cuddly and pretty
but I love my little robocat.
I call it Kit 10.

It can lie around all dozy,
all comfy cat and cosy.
It can run around the house
(chasing my computer mouse).
It has strange disgusting habits
(it can be quite rude)
but it's not the sort of cat that needs much food.
A spot of oil now and then
is all I need to give Kit 10

'cos
It's a Robocat.
It has no fur.
It has metal whiskers.
It goes whirr whirr **WHIRR.**
It's my little metal kitty
it's not cuddly and pretty
but I love my little robocat.
I call it Kit 10.

It can sneak and it can creep.
It can go beep **BEEP!**
Its eyes can flash bright red.
It can spin round on its head.
It charges round all day
then I recharge it at night –
It's the best metal moggy in the world. **ALL RIGHT!**

It's a Robocat.
It has no fur.
It has metal whiskers.
It goes whirr whirr **WHIRR.**
It's my little metal kitty
it's not cuddly and pretty
but I love my little robocat.
I call it Kit 10.

Michaela Morgan

Dark, Dark City

In a dark, dark city
There's a dark, dark street.
In the dark, dark street
There's a dark, dark house.
In the dark, dark house
There's a dark, dark room.
In the dark, dark room
There's a dark, dark cupboard.
In the dark, dark cupboard
There's a dark, dark box.
Open it up and what do you find?
The light switch
SWITCH IT ON!!

Traditional, adapted by Michaela Morgan

Vegan Delight

Ackees, chapatties
Dumplins an nan,
Channa an rotis
Onion uttapam,
Masala dosa
Green callaloo
Bhel an samosa
Corn an aloo.
Yam an cassava
Pepperpot stew,
Rotlo an guava
Rice an tofu,
Puri, paratha
Sesame casserole,
Brown eggless pasta
An brown bread rolls.

Soya milked muesli
Soya bean curd,
Soya sweet sweeties
Soya's de word,
Soya bean margarine
Soya bean sauce,
What can mek medicine?
Soya of course.

Soya meks yoghurt
Soya ice-cream,
Or soya sorbet
Soya reigns supreme,
Soya sticks liquoriced
Soya salads
Try any soya dish
Soya is bad.

Plantain an tabouli
Cornmeal pudding
Onion bhajee
Wid plenty cumin,
Breadfruit an coconuts
Molasses tea
Dairy free omelettes
Very chilli.
Ginger bread, nut roast
Sorrell, paw paw,
Cocoa an rye toast
I tek dem on tour,
Drinking cool maubi
Meks me feel sweet,
What was dat question now?
What do we eat?

Benjamin Zephaniah

Back Track, Cycle Rack

(to the tune of Nick-Nack-Paddywhack)

John ate one,
Sue ate two.
They ate picnics at the zoo.
With a lunch pack, haversack, the lion picnicked too.
First on John and then on Sue!

Lee climbed three,
Sean climbed four.
They hadn't climbed so high before.
With a chimneystack, steeplejack, never sneeze or cough.
But Lee did and blew Sean off!

Clive rode five,
Vic rode six.
Rode their bikes off to the sticks.
With a back track, cycle rack, never mind the cost.
Clive crashed his and Vic got lost!

Kevin won seven
Kate won eight.
They won goldfish at the fete.
With a pac-a-mac, thunder clap, the rain came pouring down.
Kev's fish snorkelled, Kate's fish drowned!

Di rang nine,
Ben rang ten.
Rang up all their bestest friends.
With a joke crack, have a laugh, now it's time for fun.
Our rhyme's told, our song is sung.

Maureen Haselhurst

Taking the Plunge

One day a boy said to a girl in a swimming pool 'I'm going to dive in, are you?' She replied, 'No thanks, I bet you can't anyway.' So the boy got on the diving board and dived and said, 'See.' The girl replied, 'Flipping 'eck!'

Simon Wilkinson, Margaret Wix Junior School, St Albans

Flipping 'eck, cor blimey, strewth,
You're my hero, that's the honest truth.

Lummy, crikey, lordy lord,
It's a long way down from that diving board.

Itchy beard and stone the crows,
Don't you get chlorine up your nose?

Luv a duck and strike me pink,
You're slicker than the soap in the kitchen sink.

Knock me down with a sparrow's feather,
How about us going out together?

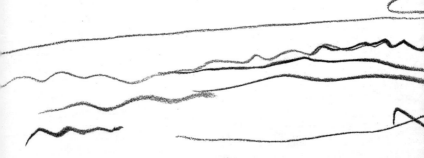

Groovy, t'riffic, brill and smashing,
Me 'n' you, we could start things splashing.

Watcha cocky, tara, see ya,
Meet me for a coke in the cafeteria.

Hallelujah and Amen,
If you like this poem you can read it again.

John Mole

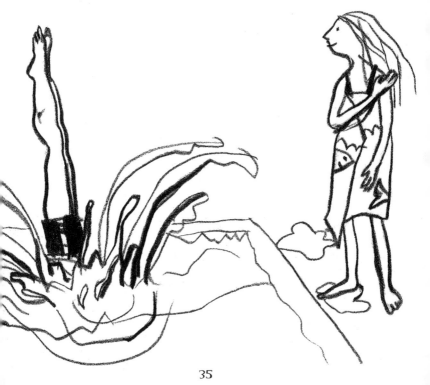

Trick or Treat

Can you give us a sweet, Mistress?
Can you give us a sweet?
We've walked for miles in the freezing breeze,
And a hot toddy and some bread and cheese
Would stop the knocking in our knees,
For we're so cold, so cold.

Can we stop for a while, Mistress?
Can we stop for a while?
We've walked for miles with some aged crones,
And a spicy drink and some buttered scones
Would ease the shaking in our bones,
For we're so cold, so cold.

Can we sit by your fire, Mistress?
Can we sit by your fire?
We've walked for miles with owls and mice,
And a hot drink and toast would suffice
To thaw the blood which has turned to ice,
For we're so cold, so cold.

Why do you start and stare, Mistress?
Why do you start and stare?
Are you amazed by our sightless eyes?
It's just a Halloween disguise,
But we must be off before sunrise,
For we're so cold, so cold.

Valerie Bloom

How to Successfully Persuade
Your Parents to Give You
More Pocket Money

Ask, request, demand, suggest, cajole or charm
Ingratiate, suck up to, flatter, compliment or smarm
Negotiate, debate, discuss, persuade, convince, explain
Or reason, justify, protest, object, dispute, complain
Propose, entreat, beseech, beg, plead, appeal, implore
Harass, go on about it, pester, whinge, whine, nag and bore
Annoy, insult, reproach, denounce, squeal, scream and shout
Go quiet, subdued, look worried, fret, brood, tremble, shiver, pout

Act depressed, downhearted, upset, snivel, sigh
Go all glum and plaintive, wobble bottom lip and cry
Sniff, sulk, grumble, stare at ceiling, mope, pine, stay in bed
Get cross, get angry, fume, seethe, fester, agitate, see red

Provoke, enrage, push, bully, aggravate and goad
Screech, smoke, burn up, ignite, spark, detonate, **EXPLODE!**

And if all that doesn't work

Here are two little tricks
That should do it with ease

No 1: smile
No 2: say please.

Andrea Shavick

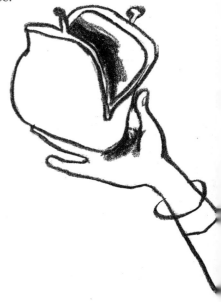

39

Rubbish

Chorus *Rubbish rubbish rubbish rubbish*
Shubby shubby shub –
SHUB it in the trash can
SHUB it in the bin
Pick a bit o' litter up and go and shub it in!

Would you like a lollipop?
Would you like a sweet?
Don't leave the sweetie wrapper lying in the street
Pop it in your pocket or
Drop it in the bin
What did we tell you?
GO AND SHUB IT IN!!!

Repeat chorus *Rubbish rubbish rubbish rubbish…*

Don't eat your fish and chips and
Throw the paper down
Don't leave your cola tins
Rattling round the town
Snatch 'em up and catch 'em up and
Throw them in a bin
What did we tell you?
GO AND SHUB IT IN!!!

Repeat chorus *Rubbish rubbish rubbish rubbish…*

So –
DON'T be a litter bug
Take a look around
What can you see here
Lying on the ground?
Sweep it up or pick it up and
Toss it in the bin
WHAT DID WE TELL YOU?
GO AND SHUB IT IN!!!

Vivian French

Stuffed!

Tortelloni, tortelloni.
Eat it, feed it to your pony.

Pasta pesto, pasta pesto.
Put it in the pan. Hey presto!

Tagliatelle, tagliatelle.
Stuff yourself. Fill your belly.
(Eat it while you're watching telly.)

Macaroni, macaroni.
Eat it and you won't be bony.

Fish and chips. Fish and chips.
Cool. Yeah cool! (Lick your lips.)

Sausage and mash. Sausage and mash.
Dollop of ketchup? Just a dash.

Ravioli. Ravioli.
Second helping. Bless my soul(y).

Yoghurt, chocolate mousse or ice cream
All together (that's a nice dream!)

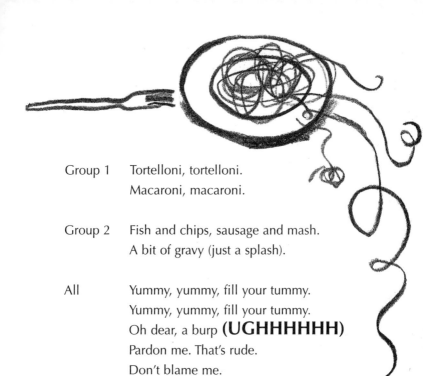

| Group 1 | Tortelloni, tortelloni. |
| | Macaroni, macaroni. |

| Group 2 | Fish and chips, sausage and mash. |
| | A bit of gravy (just a splash). |

All	Yummy, yummy, fill your tummy.
	Yummy, yummy, fill your tummy.
	Oh dear, a burp **(UGHHHHHH)**
	Pardon me. That's rude.
	Don't blame me.
	Blame all that food.

Tom Crabtree

43

Ghost Train

Chorus *On the g-g-g-g-g-g-g-g-ghost train,*
it was dark, it was scary, it was insane,
and I'm never going back there ever again
on the g-g-g-g-g-g-g-g-ghost train.

It's a lot of fun, my big brother said,
skeletons, ghosts and a man with his head
tucked under his arm, but you needn't look,
I've been here before, so I sat and I shook

Repeat *On the g-g-g-g-g-g-g-g-ghost train...*
chorus

I didn't like it, not one bit,
webs hung down from the ceiling and hit
the side of your face as you travelled past
ever so slowly, oh can't we go fast?

Repeat *On the g-g-g-g-g-g-g-g-ghost train...*
chorus

Coffin lids creaked and a skeleton fell
across our path and I let out a yell.
Its echo bounced round the tunnel and back
like a scream from a raving maniac

Repeat *On the g-g-g-g-g-g-g-g-ghost train...*
chorus

44

Back out in the open I just couldn't shift
my brother pulled and then tried to lift
me out, but nothing worked till he said,
'Let's have another go instead...'

I jumped to my feet and staggered away,
my brother said, 'Maybe another day.'
But no, no way could I ever face
another trip through that terrible place,

Chorus   *On the g-g-g-g-g-g-g-g-ghost train,*
it was dark, it was scary, it was insane,
and I'm never going back there ever again
on the g-g-g-g-g-g-g-g-ghost train.

Brian Moses

45

The Ballad of Killer Kincaid

Miss Kelly Kincaid's our teacher's name
I'll tell you the story of her rise to fame.
Fifteen animals she's lost or mislaid;
Throughout the school she's called: Killer Kincaid.

Killer Kincaid, Killer Kincaid,
They call our teacher Killer Kincaid.

Don't go thinking she's a hard-hearted dame;
Never hurt a child, never used the cane.
But pets are different. I don't why, but
If she goes near them, they just up and die.

Killer Kincaid, Killer Kincaid,
They call our teacher Killer Kincaid.

Homer, the hamster, was the first to go.
And how it happened, we just don't know.
You can't blame Miss; she was having her meal
When Homer got trapped inside his wheel.

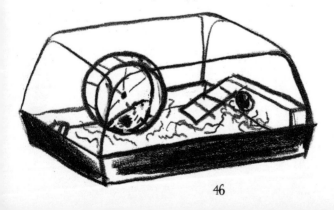

Killer Kincaid, Killer Kincaid,
Find Mr Benson, borrow his spade.
Dig a small hole, say a short prayer.
The cage sits empty, no pet there.

Bill's rabbit, Fluff, was next to pass away,
And Milly the Mouse, escaped the same day.
Then Gazza, the guinea pig, died of fright
When the caretaker's cat got in one night.

Killer Kincaid, Killer Kincaid,
They call our teacher Killer Kincaid.

I'm sure Miss Kincaid didn't mean to shout,
And the gerbil was old; its heart gave out.
We'd had the goldfish for years and years,
But they don't last long once the food disappears.

Killer Kincaid, Killer Kincaid,
Find Mr Benson, borrow his spade.
Dig a small hole, say a short prayer.
The bowl sits empty, no pet there.

Poor Miss Kincaid, hangs her head in shame.
Can't understand how she got this bad name.
She's just a bit careless; she's had bad luck.
Poor Miss Kincaid, the name has just stuck.

Killer Kincaid, Killer Kincaid.
Don't call our teacher Killer Kincaid.

Rose Impey

Hello Sir

Hello sir. *Hello sir.*
Meet you at the grocer?
No sir. Why sir?
Because I've got a cold sir.
Where'd you get the cold sir?
At the North Pole sir
How many did you catch sir?
One, sir, two, sir, three, sir, four, sir
  there weren't any more sir.

Do you want some pie, sir?
Not if I will die, sir.
Just spit out the germs, sir.
And eat up all the worms, sir.
One, sir, two, sir, three, sir, four, sir
  can you eat some more, sir?

Traditional, adapted by Michaela Morgan

Buzz Buzz

Bees on your fingers,
Bees on your toes,
Bees in your ear-holes
And bees up your nose.

Bees on your tongue-tip,
Bees between your teeth,
Bees, bees on top of bees
And bees underneath.

Bees in your toothpaste,
Bees on your brush,
Bees going **BOOM BOOM!**
And bees going hush.

Bees on your Weetabix,
Bees wearing boots,
Bees wearing T-shirts
And bees in best suits.

Bees up the chimney,
Bees down the drain,
Bees bumping into bees,
Oh not bees again!

Bees in your school-bag,
Bees in your bed,
Bees live a buzzy life
Then

        drop

            down

                dead.

John Mole

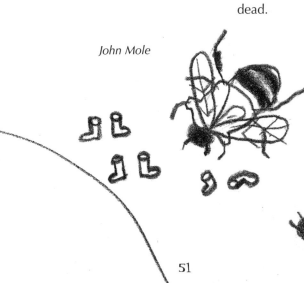

Dog in the Playground

Dog in the playground
Suddenly there.
Smile on his face,
Tail in the air.

Dog in the playground
Bit of a fuss:
I know that dog –
Lives next to us!

Dog in the playground:
Oh, no he don't.
He'll come with me,
You see if he won't.

The word gets round;
The crowd gets bigger.
His name's Bob.
It ain't – it's Trigger.

They call him Archie!
They call him Frank!
Lives by the Fish Shop!
Lives up the Bank!
Who told you that?
Pipe down! Shut up!
I know that dog
Since he was a pup.

Dog in the playground:
We'll catch him, Miss.
Leave it to us.
Just watch this!

Dog in the playground
What a to-do!
Thirty-five children,
Caretaker too,
Chasing the dog,
Chasing each other.
I know that dog –
He's our dog's brother!

We've cornered him now;
He can't get away.
Told you we'd catch him,
Robert and – Hey!
Don't open that door –
Oh, Glenis, you fool!
Look, Miss, what's happened:
Dog in the school.

Dog in the classroom,
Dog in the hall,
Dog in the toilets –
He's paying a call!
Forty-six children,
Caretaker too,
Headmaster, three teachers,
Hullabaloo!

Lost him! Can't find him!
He's vanished! And then:
Look, Miss, he's back
In the playground again.

Shouting and shoving –
I'll give you what for! –
Sixty-five children
Head for the door.

Dog in the playground,
Smile on his face,
Tail in the air,
Winning the race.

Dog in his element
Off at a jog,
Out of the gates:
Wish I was a dog.

Dog in the playground:
Couldn't he run?

Dog in the playground
        ...Gone!

Allan Ahlberg

Oo Oo!

A woman in a churchyard sat
Oo Oo!
She wore her coat and a flowery hat
Oo Oo!

She heard a rustling in the trees
Oo Oo!
Was it an owl? Was it the breeze?
Oo Oo!

She saw three coffins carried in
Oo Oo!
very long and very thin
Oo Oo!

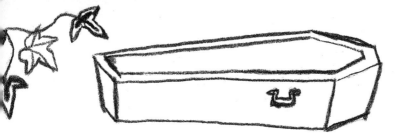

She knocked on the coffin 1 2 3
Oo Oo!
Will anybody talk to me?
Oo Oo!

She heard a groaning loud and clear
Oo Oo!
Something was creeping up to her
Oo Oo!

She felt the touch of an icy claw
Oo Oo!
She ran away and was seen no more
Oo Oo!

Traditional, adapted by Michaela Morgan

Bully in a Lorry — Out of My Way

Eighteen wheels pounding down the motorway
Eighteen wheels rolling down the road
Eighteen wheels travelling every which way
Eighteen wheels powering the load.

I'm a bully in a lorry and I'm always in a hurry
I'm a bully in a lorry and I never say sorry
I'm a bully in a lorry full of slurry from Bury
I'm a bully in a lorry and I never say sorry.

Concrete to Cardiff
Stacks of steel to Sunderland
Bags of bricks to Basildon
Rolls of rags to Rotherham
Out of my way!   Pedal to the metal!
Out of my way!   Drive drive drive!
Out of my way!   Moving up behind you!
Out of my way!   Doing 95!

Eighteen wheels hammering the tarmac
Eighteen wheels giving it some gas
Eighteen wheels thunder down the black track
Eighteen wheels nobody gets past.

I'm a bully in a lorry, hotter than a curry
I'm a bully in a lorry, you'd better start to worry
I'm a bully in a lorry in a hurry and a flurry
I'm a bully in a lorry and I never say sorry.

Chicken sheds from Chippenham
Widgets from Warrington
Piles of pipes from Penzance
Tons of tea to Tenby
Out of my way!   Pedal to the metal!
Out of my way!   Drive drive drive!
Out of my way!   Moving up behind you!
Out of my way!   Doing 95!

Eighteen wheels pounding down the motorway
Eighteen wheels rolling down the road
Eighteen wheels travelling every which way
Eighteen wheels powering the load.

Get out of my way!

David Harmer and Paul Cookson

My Dad Is Very Keen on Sport

My Dad may be **OLD**
But he's still keen on sport –
WATCHING IT is bliss!
He's had installed cable TV
To make sure he does not miss
A single
football match goal
　　cricketer's bowl
　　　　downhill ski
　　　　　　golf match tee
　　　　　　　runner's sprint
　　　　　　　　ice-skate glint
　　　　　　　　judo throw
　　　　　　　　　rower's row
　　　　　　　　　　rider's jump
　　　　　　　　　　　stockcar's bump
　　　　　　　　　　　　swimmer's stroke
　　　　　　　　　　　　engine's choke
　　　　　　　　　　　　　basketball score
　　　　　　　　　　　　　　or rugby crowd's roar!

BUT after five minutes
He falls asleep
In his armchair.

My Dad is living proof that
Although sport may be **INSPIRING**
It's also **VERY** tiring...!

Trevor Harvey

Index of titles and first lines

First lines are in italics

Index of authors

Acknowledgements

Allan Ahlberg: 'Dog in the Playground' from *Please Mrs Butler* by Allan Ahlberg (Kestrel, 1983) copyright © Allan Ahlberg, 1983. **Ros Barber**: 'Crocodile under My Bed' © Ros Barber. **Valerie Bloom**: 'Trick or Treat' © Valerie Bloom. **Tom Crabtree**: 'Stuffed!' © Tom Crabtree. **Vivian French**: 'The Bee's Story' and 'Rubbish' © Vivian French. **David Harmer**: 'Daredevil Gran' © David Harmer. **David Harmer and Paul Cookson**: 'Bully in a Lorry – Out of My Way' © David Harmer and Paul Cookson. **Trevor Harvey**: 'My Dad Is Very Keen on Sport' © Trevor Harvey, first published in *Fun with Poems*, edited by Irene Yates (Brilliant Publications, 2000); reprinted by permission of Trevor Harvey. **Maureen Haselhurst**: 'Back Track, Cycle Rack' © Maureen Haselhurst, 2000. **Rose Impey**: 'The Ballad of Killer Kincaid' © Rose Impey. **John Mole**: 'Buzz Buzz' and 'Taking the Plunge' © John Mole, both first published in *Boo to a Goose* (Peterloo Poets, 1987). **Michaela Morgan**: 'Dark, Dark City', 'Hello Sir', 'Kit 10', 'Mrs Sprockett's Strange Machine', 'Oo Oo!' and 'Words to Whisper' © Michaela Morgan. **Brian Moses**: 'Ghost Train' © Brian Moses, first published in *Knock Down Ginger and Other Poems* (Cambridge University Press, 1994). **Tom Murphy**: 'Monster Pie' © Tom Murphy. **Nick Penny**: 'What Do You Do with a Didgeridoo?' and 'Silly Billy Banjo' © Nick Penny, 2000. **Andrea Shavick**: 'How to Successfully Persuade Your Parents to Give You More Pocket Money' © Andrea Shavick, first published in *Unzip Your Lips Again* (Macmillan, 1999). 'My Old Man' © Andrea Shavick. **Nick Toczek**: 'Rat in the Attic' © Nick Toczek. An alternative version was first published in *Never Stare at a Grizzly Bear* by Nick Toczek (Macmillan, 2000). **Benjamin Zephaniah**: 'Vegan Delight' from *Talking Turkeys* by Benjamin Zephaniah (Viking, 1994) copyright © Benjamin Zephaniah, 1994.

Every effort has been made to contact copyright holders. The publishers would like to hear from any copyright holder not acknowledged.